MESSAGES

FROM

ALLAH

VOLUME – II

HIDAYAH PUBLISHERS

DEAR,

_____

_____

_____

Messages From Allah – Volume I
ISBN 978-1-998843-41-1

Messages From Allah – Volume II
ISBN 978-1-998843-42-8

LIST OF STORIES

ZAYNAB & ZAMIR'S JOURNEY OF FAITH

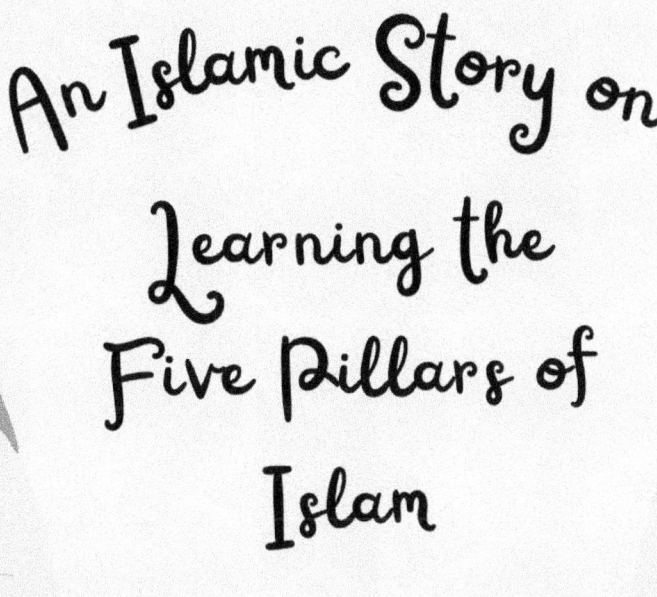

An Islamic Story on Learning the Five Pillars of Islam

THE SHAHADAH GATE

Zaynab and her best friend, Zamir, were two peas in a pod; they both loved adventure! Whether it was climbing trees, exploring attics, or just dreaming up wild stories, they were always on the lookout for excitement.

One sunny afternoon, they were under their favorite tree, munching on apples and swapping stories, when Zaynab spoke up. "Zamir," she said, her eyes sparkling with curiosity, "I want to learn more about Islam. Like, I know we pray and fast, but why? What does it all mean?"

Zamir nodded. "Yeah, me too! What does it really mean to be Muslim?"

Just then, a beautiful butterfly with shimmering wings landed on Zaynab's knee. It flapped its wings and, to their surprise, spoke!

"Hello, Zaynab and Zamir," the butterfly said in a soft, tinkly voice. "Your wish to learn has been heard! An amazing journey awaits you— a quest to discover the wonders of Islam!"

Zaynab and Zamir gasped. A talking butterfly! This was even better than their usual adventures!

The butterfly fluttered upward, leaving a trail of sparkling dust that formed a path in the air. "Follow me!" it called.

Without a moment's hesitation, Zaynab and Zamir jumped up and followed the magical butterfly. The path led them away from everything familiar, through fields bursting with flowers and over sparkling streams. Finally, they stopped in front of a magnificent gate covered in beautiful designs and shimmering stars.

The gate seemed to shimmer and glow, as if inviting them to step through. As they got closer, Zaynab noticed that the designs weren't just random; they were 'words' written in beautiful, flowing Arabic script.

"Welcome to the Land of Faith!" the butterfly announced. "Here, you'll learn about the first pillar of Islam—'Shahadah'. It means believing that there is only one God, Allah, and that Prophet Muhammad, peace be upon him, is His last messenger."

The Messenger of Allah (P.B.U.H) said,

"Verily, whoever testifies there is no God but Allah, then Allah will forbid him from entering Hellfire and require him to enter Paradise." [Sahih Ibn Hibban 199]

The gate swung open with a quiet whoosh, revealing a breathtaking world. Lush gardens burst with colorful flowers, their sweet fragrance carried on the breeze. Majestic mountains soared into the sky, their peaks hidden by fluffy clouds.

But as Zaynab and Zamir stepped through the gate, they realized something wasn't quite right. The air felt heavy and dark, and shadowy doubts seemed to cloud the sky. The path ahead was hazy, lost in mist.

Whispers, carried on the wind, reached their ears.

"Is there really just one God?"

"How can we be sure about things we can't even see?"

Zaynab and Zamir exchanged a worried look. They'd had those same questions themselves!

The butterfly, sensing their fear, fluttered closer. "Don't be afraid," it reassured them. "These doubts are challenges. You have to face them to make your faith stronger! And remember, Allah is always with you, even if you can't see Him."

Taking a deep breath, Zaynab and Zamir started down the path, determined to keep going. Soon, they came to a shady clearing, where a kind-looking old man with a long white beard sat beneath a tree. He smiled at them.

"Welcome, young travelers," he said. "I'm here to guide you on your journey of faith."

Zaynab and Zamir poured out their questions and doubts to the old man, who listened patiently with a knowing smile.

"Ah, yes," he said when they were finished. "It's true that we can't see Allah with our eyes. But we can see evidence of Him all around us!"

He gestured toward the beautiful landscape. "Look at those flowers, those mountains, that vast sky! Do you think all of this just happened by accident? Just like a painting needs a painter, this incredible world needs a Creator. And that Creator is Allah (S.W.T)."

The old man went on to explain that the Quran, Islam's holy book, teaches about Allah's oneness and is full of examples of His power and wisdom.

"Think about the sun and moon, day and night, the birds and the fish," he said. "They all follow a perfect system, created by Allah (S.W.T)."

"But what about believing in things we can't see?" Zamir asked.

The old man smiled again. "We believe in things like love, kindness, and honesty, right? We can't see those things, but we can feel them in our hearts. Faith is like that, too. It's something we feel; a connection with Allah that grows stronger the more we learn about Him and the amazing world He created."

Zaynab and Zamir listened closely. The old man's words made sense! They came to understand that being Muslim was not only about belief but also about actions. It was about trusting in Allah, being kind, and trying their best to be good people.

As they continued their journey through the Land of Faith, the shadowy doubts began to fade away, and the path ahead became clearer. Zaynab and Zamir felt a sense of peace, knowing they were on the right track. Their adventure was just beginning, and they were excited to see what other amazing things they would learn!

THE LAND OF PRAYER

With their hearts full and their faith stronger than ever, Zaynab and Zamir continued their adventure. The Land of Faith shifted and changed around them as they walked. Towering mountains gave way to rolling hills, and the lush gardens transformed into peaceful meadows.

Soon, they came to a beautiful mosque. Its minaret stretched towards the sky, and its dome shimmered in the sunlight. The melodious sound of the Adhan, the call to prayer, filled the air.

"Welcome to the Land of Prayer (Salah)," the butterfly announced. "Here, you'll learn about Salat, the second pillar of Islam; praying five times a day."

Zaynab and Zamir had always prayed with their families, but they'd never really understood why they prayed at certain times, or what each prayer meant.

As they stepped inside the mosque, a kind Imam with a warm smile greeted them. "Welcome, young travelers," he said. "It makes me happy to see you so eager to learn about prayer. Salat is a special way for us to connect with Allah, to thank Him for all He gives us, and to ask for His guidance. The Prophet Muhammad (P.B.U.H) said: 'The key to Paradise is Salat, and the key to Salat is Wudu'.'"

The Imam explained that there are five daily prayers: Fajr (at dawn), Dhuhr (midday), Asr (afternoon), Maghrib (sunset), and Isha (night). Each prayer has a certain number of rakats—units of prayer—and they are performed facing the Kaaba in Mecca, the holiest site in Islam.

"But why these times?" Zaynab asked. "Is there a reason we pray at these specific times of day?"

"That's a wonderful question," the Imam said, beaming at her. "Allah, in His infinite wisdom, has given us these prayer times as a gift. It's a chance to pause throughout our busy days and reconnect with Him. Fajr is a time to start the day with gratitude. Dhuhr is a break in the middle of our work and play. Asr reminds us to slow down as the day winds down. Maghrib is a time to reflect as the sun sets. And Isha'a helps us to clear our minds and prepare for a peaceful sleep."

He showed Zaynab and Zamir the movements for each prayer and taught them the words, explaining the meaning behind everything they did.

"When we stand to pray," the Imam said, "we stand before Allah with humility and respect. When we bow, we are showing our submission to Him. And when we prostrate, our foreheads touching the ground, it is the ultimate sign of surrender and devotion."

Zaynab and Zamir practiced the prayers with the Imam. They experienced a gentle and soothing feeling of peace as if all their worries had been washed away.

They realized that prayer wasn't just about going through the motions; it was about connecting with Allah, clearing their minds, and focusing on what was truly important.

The Messenger of Allah (P.B.U.H) stated:

"The place of prayer (Salah) in religion is like the place of the head in the body." [Majmau'l-Awsat, 3:154]

As Zaynab and Zamir left the mosque, the butterfly led them on a test—a test of their commitment to prayer!

First, they came across a group of children playing tag. Zaynab and Zamir really wanted to join in, but it was almost time for Dhuhr prayer.

"Come on, just one game!" the children called out. "You can pray later!"

Zaynab and Zamir hesitated. It was really tempting... But then they remembered what the Imam had said about putting Salat first.

"Thanks, but we need to pray now," Zaynab said. "We can play after!"

The children were disappointed, but they understood. Zaynab and Zamir found a quiet spot nearby and prayed Dhuhr. Afterward, they felt inner peace for putting Allah (S.W.T) first.

Next, they passed a bakery. Oh, the smells! Warm, sweet, delicious smells! Zaynab and Zamir's stomachs rumbled. They really wanted to try those yummy-looking treats! But it was time for Asr prayer.

They found a little garden behind the bakery and prayed Asr Salah there. Just as they finished, the baker came out with a big smile and handed them each a warm pastry.

"I saw you both praying," he said. "May Allah bless you for your devotion."

Zaynab and Zamir realized that even though they chose prayer first, they still got to enjoy the treats, and they tasted even better knowing they'd done the right thing!

As they continued on their journey, more challenges popped up. Sometimes they felt lazy, or tired, or rushed... but every time, they remembered how important Salat was. They made the effort to connect with Allah (S.W.T), no matter what.

By the end of their time in the Land of Prayer, Zaynab and Zamir understood just how special Salat really was. It wasn't just something they had to do; it was a gift, a way to find peace and guidance. They knew that no matter what adventures life threw their way, Salat would always be a part of their lives.

THE LAND OF CHARITY

Zaynab and Zamir felt grateful for everything they'd learned about prayer as they left the Land of Prayer. Their magical journey continued, the landscape shifting around them once more. Peaceful meadows gave way to busy towns and bustling villages, full of people going about their daily lives.

"Welcome to the Land of Charity," announced the butterfly. "Here, you'll discover Zakat; the third pillar of Islam. It's about sharing what you have with those in need."

Zaynab and Zamir's parents often gave money or clothes to charity, but the children didn't really understand what Zakat was all about, or why it was so important.

They soon came to a bustling community center. Volunteers were busy sorting clothes, packing boxes with food, and cooking a big pot of something delicious.

A kind woman with a warm smile greeted them. "Welcome!" she said. "We're so glad you're here. Today, we're distributing Zakat to families who need it. Would you like to help?"

Zaynab and Zamir were eager to lend a hand. They sorted clothes by size, packed boxes with essential food items, and even helped stir a giant pot of lentil soup!

As they worked, the woman explained the importance of Zakat. "In Islam," she said, "we believe that everything we have is a gift from Allah. Zakat is a way to show our thankfulness for those gifts by sharing what we have with people who are struggling."

"And establish prayer and give Zakat, and whatever good you put forward for yourselves – you will find it with Allah."
[Surah Al-Baqarah, 2:110]

She went on to explain that Zakat isn't just about money. It's about sharing your time, your skills—anything you can offer to make someone else's life a little bit better.

The Messenger of Allah (P.B.U.H) said:

"There is no envy except in two: a person whom Allah has given wealth and he spends it in the right way, and a person whom Allah has given wisdom (i. e. religious knowledge) and he gives his decisions accordingly and teaches it to the others." [Sahih Bukhari, V: 2, B: 24, 490]

"It's about caring for your community and making sure everyone has what they need," she said.

Zaynab and Zamir listened, their hearts growing full. They realized that Zakat wasn't just a rule; it was a beautiful way to be kind and help others!

As Zaynab and Zamir traveled through the Land of Charity, they faced little tests—tests of their generosity.

First, they saw a young boy sitting alone by the road. His clothes were torn, and tears streamed down his face. He told them he'd lost his parents and had nowhere to go.

Zaynab and Zamir felt a pang of sadness. They wanted to help, but they only had a few coins and some snacks left in their bags.

"It's not much," Zaynab said, "but we can share what we have."

They gave the boy their snacks and their coins. His face lit up, and he thanked them with a shy smile. He shared the snacks with them, and they sat together for a while, talking and laughing like old friends. It wasn't much, but Zaynab and Zamir realized that even small acts of kindness could make a big difference.

Later, they saw an old woman struggling to carry a heavy basket. Zaynab and Zamir rushed over to help, carrying the basket all the way to her house. They even helped her unpack her groceries!

"May Allah bless you, children," the woman said. "You've been such a help!"

Zaynab and Zamir felt a warm glow inside. They realized that helping others wasn't just about giving things—it was about offering a hand, a kind word, or just listening to someone who needed it.

They continued on their journey, and with every step, they found more opportunities to share and care. They volunteered at a soup kitchen where people who were hungry could get a hot meal. They donated their old toys to an orphanage, so other children could enjoy them. They even helped clean up a park, making it beautiful for everyone!

With every act of kindness, their hearts grew bigger, and they felt closer to Allah (S.W.T) and their community.

By the end of their time in the Land of Charity, Zaynab and Zamir understood that giving wasn't about how much you had, but about how much you cared. It felt good to help others, and they knew that Zakat wasn't just a rule; it was a way to spread kindness and love. Wherever their adventures took them next, they would carry the spirit of generosity in their hearts.

THE LAND OF FASTING

Zaynab and Zamir left the Land of Charity with full hearts, understanding just how important it was to share and care for others. The landscape shifted around them once more, the bustling towns and villages fading away. They found themselves surrounded by peaceful deserts and serene oases. The air was calm and quiet.

"Welcome to the Land of Fasting," the butterfly announced. "Here, you will learn about Sawm, the fourth pillar of Islam. It means abstaining from food and drink from dawn until sunset during the holy month of Ramadan."

Zaynab and Zamir had fasted before during Ramadan, but it wasn't easy! They were still young, and it was really hard to resist the yummy snacks and refreshing drinks.

They came to a beautiful oasis, where a wise-looking sheikh greeted them with a warm smile.

"Welcome, young travelers," he said. "Ramadan is a special time for Muslims everywhere. It is a time for reflection, for self-control, and for drawing closer to Allah (S.W.T). Allah's Messenger (P.B.U.H) said, "Fasting is a shield. So, the person observing fasting should not behave thoughtlessly and impolitely, and if somebody fights with him or abuses him, he should tell him twice, 'I am fasting.'"

The sheikh explained that fasting wasn't just about giving up food and drink; it was about purifying your heart and mind, too.

"When we fast," he said, "we learn to control our desires, to be patient, and to focus on what's truly important. It is a time to strengthen our connection with Allah and to remember those who are less fortunate than ourselves."

Zaynab and Zamir listened carefully. They were starting to understand that fasting was about much more than just feeling hungry and thirsty. It was a test of willpower, a way to become more disciplined, and a chance to grow closer to Allah (S.W.T).

The Land of Fasting had its challenges—especially for two young adventurers who loved yummy snacks!

First, Zaynab and Zamir came across a fruit vendor with a cart piled high with colorful, delicious-smelling fruits. Juicy mangoes, sweet grapes, watermelon... Zaynab and Zamir's mouths started to water just looking at them! Oh, how they wished they could take a bite, or even just a sip of cool water! But they remembered the sheikh's words about patience and self-control. Taking a deep breath, they closed their eyes for a moment and kept walking.

Later, they passed by a group of children playing a lively game of soccer. Zaynab and Zamir loved soccer! Their feet itched to join in, to run and kick the ball alongside the other kids. But they knew that if they got hot and tired, their fast would be even harder.

So they waved to the children and kept going, reminding themselves that the joy of breaking their fast at sunset would be even sweeter if they stayed committed.

As the day wore on, the sun beat down, hot and intense. Zaynab and Zamir's throats were parched. They stumbled upon a small, hidden oasis; a cluster of palm trees surrounding a pool of cool, inviting water. The temptation to scoop up a handful and drink deeply was almost unbearable.

But they remembered why they were fasting. They thought about people all over the world who didn't have enough food or clean water, and they felt grateful for the blessings in their own lives. Instead of drinking from the oasis, they sat quietly in the shade of the palm trees, enjoying the coolness and the gentle sound of the breeze rustling the leaves.

Finally, the sun began to set, painting the sky in shades of orange and pink. As Zaynab and Zamir broke their fasts, they felt a sense of accomplishment and a deep inner peace. They had faced the challenges of fasting with courage and determination, and their faith had grown stronger because of it.

As the sun dipped below the horizon, painting the sky in breathtaking hues of orange and purple, Zaynab and Zamir returned to the sheikh's oasis, their hearts full of peace.

The sheikh greeted them with a warm smile and offered them dates and cool water to break their fast. As they ate and drank, they told him about all the challenges they'd faced and how they'd managed to resist temptation.

"You have done well, young travelers," the sheikh said, his eyes twinkling kindly. "You have learned valuable lessons about self-control, patience, and empathy. The true reward of fasting is not just the food and drink we enjoy at sunset, but the spiritual growth and closeness to Allah that we achieve. The Prophet (P.B.U.H) said, 'There is a gate in Paradise called Ar-Raiyan, and those who observe fasts will enter through it on the Day of Resurrection and none except them will enter through it. It will be said, 'Where are those who used to observe fasts?' They will get up, and none except them will enter through it. After their entry, the gate will be closed and nobody will enter through it.'"

Zaynab and Zamir nodded, their hearts overflowing with gratitude. They understood now that fasting wasn't just a physical act; it was a journey of the spirit. A journey that had brought them closer to Allah (S.W.T) and helped them understand themselves and the world around them a little better. They would strive to be more patient, more compassionate, and more grateful, not just during Ramadan, but every single day.

THE LAND OF PILGRIMAGE

Zaynab and Zamir felt the warmth of spiritual growth glowing inside them as they left the Land of Fasting, their hearts full of gratitude for everything they'd learned. The desert landscape faded away, replaced by a vast, open plain. And in the distance, shining under the golden sun, they saw a magnificent city.

"Welcome to the Land of Pilgrimage," announced the butterfly. "Here, you'll learn about Hajj, the fifth pillar of Islam. It is a special journey to the holy city of Mecca that every Muslim who is able should try to make at least once in their life."

Zaynab and Zamir had heard stories about Hajj from their families, and they were both excited and a little bit nervous to see it for themselves.

As they entered the bustling city of Mecca, a friendly young scholar greeted them. "Welcome, travelers," he said. "Hajj is a time for unity, equality, and spiritual renewal. Muslims from all over the world come here, dressed in simple white clothing, to perform the same rituals and stand before Allah (S.W.T) as equals."

The scholar pointed to a large, cube-shaped building in the center of a courtyard. "That is the Kaaba," he explained. "Muslims all over the world face towards it when they pray Salah." He told them the story of how the Prophet Ibrahim (A.S) and his son, Ismael (A.S), built the Kaaba as a symbol of worshipping only Allah Al-Mighty.

He described the rituals of Hajj: walking around the Kaaba, running between the hills of Safa and Marwa, standing in prayer on the plain of Arafat, and throwing pebbles at three pillars that represent rejecting temptation.

"Hajj is a journey of a lifetime," the scholar said. "It's a chance to forget about worldly distractions, to ask for forgiveness, and to grow closer to Allah. The Prophet (P.B.U.H) said, 'Whoever performs Hajj for Allah's pleasure ..., and does not do evil or sins then he will return (after Hajj free from all sins) as if he were born anew.' [Sahih Al-Bukhari, 1521]"

As Zaynab and Zamir followed the scholar through the crowds, they witnessed the incredible diversity of the Muslim community. Everywhere they looked, they saw people! People of all different colors, speaking different languages, wearing different clothes. It was like the whole world had gathered in one place!

Zaynab and Zamir were amazed by the sense of unity and brotherhood all around them. They realized that even though they came from different countries and spoke different languages, they were all part of one big family—the Muslim Ummah—connected by their shared faith in Allah (S.W.T) and Prophet Muhammad (P.B.U.H).

They saw pilgrims helping each other, sharing food and water, and praying together. Kindness and compassion seemed to be everywhere! Zaynab and Zamir felt a warm sense of belonging, grateful to be a part of something so much bigger than themselves.

Zaynab and Zamir's journey through the Land of Pilgrimage was coming to an end. They stood on a hill overlooking the vast plain of Arafat, where thousands upon thousands of pilgrims stood in prayer. The setting sun painted the sky in brilliant colors, and a feeling of peace settled over Zaynab and Zamir.

They realized that this incredible adventure had been about so much more than just visiting different places. It had been a journey of self-discovery, a journey that had helped them understand their faith and themselves a little better. They had learned about the five pillars of Islam, witnessed the beauty and diversity of the Muslim community, and felt the power of shared faith.

With grateful hearts and minds buzzing with new knowledge, they thanked the butterfly for guiding them.

The butterfly smiled. "Remember," it said, "the journey of faith never really ends. Keep learning, keep growing, and share the beauty of Islam with everyone you meet."

And with a flutter of its shimmering wings, the butterfly disappeared.

Zaynab and Zamir found themselves back under their favorite tree, blinking in the warm sunshine. They looked at each other, their eyes shining with newfound wisdom and understanding. Their adventure might be over, but their journey of faith was just beginning.

Zaynab and Zamir knew they would never forget this amazing adventure or the lessons they had learned. They would continue praying Salah with devotion, sharing generously with others, and fasting with discipline. They also dreamed of one day making the pilgrimage to Mecca themselves.

But most importantly, they would carry the spirit of Islam with them always, spreading kindness, compassion, and understanding wherever they went.

Zaynab and Zamir returned to their everyday lives, but they weren't the same. They were changed. They told everyone about their adventure and everything they had learned. They wanted everyone to discover the beauty and peace of Islam for themselves!

As they grew older, Zaynab and Zamir became leaders in their communities, always remembering the lessons they had learned on their journey. They shared the messages of peace, unity, and love, hoping to inspire others to embark on their own journeys of faith.

The Messenger of Allah (P.B.U.H) said:

"Islam has been built on five [pillars]: testifying that there is no god but Allah and that Muhammad is the Messenger of Allah, performing the prayers, paying the zakah, making the pilgrimage to the House, and fasting in Ramadan."
[Al-Bukhari and Muslim]

YUSUF
AND THE
LOST
LAMB

An Islamic Story on
Seeking Forgiveness
& Having Faith in
Allah's Plan

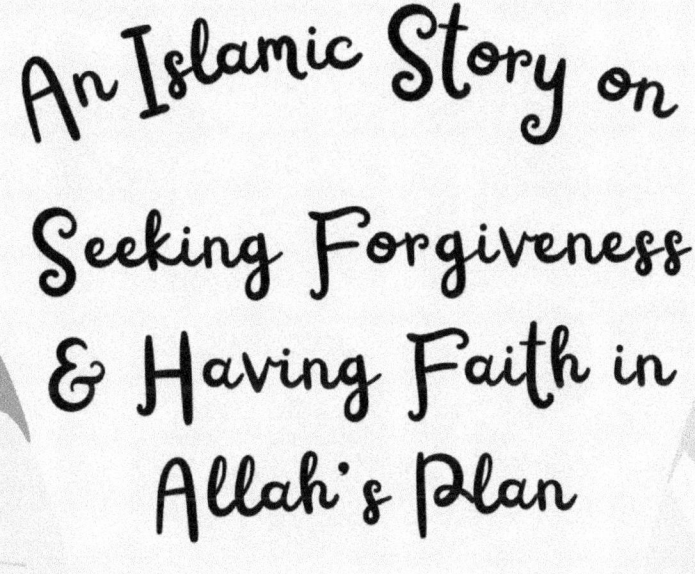

RAHMA GOES MISSING

The sun peeked over the hills, chasing away the night shadows and painting the valley in warm, golden light. A gentle breeze whispered through the trees, carrying the sweet scent of wildflowers. It was a perfect morning for a shepherd, and young Yusuf was already out with his flock.

Yusuf was known throughout the village for being responsible and caring. He looked after his sheep as if they were his family, always making sure they had plenty of grass to eat and cool, clear water to drink. But there was one sheep—a playful little lamb named 'Rahma' that held a special place in his heart. With her soft, brown eyes and gentle bleating, she was as dear to him as a sister.

As the sun climbed higher in the sky, Yusuf led his flock to a lush, green meadow. The sheep spread out, happily munching on the juicy grass. Yusuf sat down in the shade of a large tree, his eyes scanning the flock, always watchful. Rahma, as always, was a little ball of energy, bouncing around and playfully head-butting the other sheep.

Suddenly, a flash of color caught Yusuf's eye. A beautiful butterfly with wings like stained glass flitted past, dancing from one flower to the next. Mesmerized by its beauty, Yusuf forgot all about his sheep for a moment.

When the butterfly finally fluttered away, disappearing behind a clump of trees, Yusuf blinked and turned his attention back to his flock. And that's when his heart skipped a beat. He counted the sheep once, twice... Rahma was gone!

Yusuf's heart leaped into his throat. Fear, sudden and sharp, pricked at him. He jumped to his feet and scanned the meadow, his heart pounding.

"Rahma!" he called out, his voice tight with worry. "Rahma, where are you?"

Yusuf searched everywhere. He checked all of Rahma's favorite spots: behind the bushes, under the trees, near the sparkling stream. But Rahma was nowhere to be found. The meadow, usually filled with the sounds of bleating sheep, was eerily silent.

Minutes passed, stretching into what felt like hours. Anxious thoughts gripped Yusuf's heart, gradually turning into a piercing fear. He imagined Rahma lost and scared, calling out for him. What if she had wandered into the dark forest at the edge of the meadow, the one full of wild animals?

"It's my fault," he thought, tears stinging his eyes. "I wasn't paying attention. I should have been watching her more closely."

He remembered his grandfather's words: *A shepherd is responsible for his flock. He has to protect them from harm.* Yusuf had failed. And now Rahma was paying the price.

He sank to his knees, burying his face in his hands. Guilt pressed down on him like a heavy stone. The meadow, once so peaceful and familiar, now seemed vast and scary. Even the chirping of birds sounded like whispers of blame.

But Yusuf knew he couldn't give up. He had to find Rahma. Wiping his eyes, he took a deep breath and stood up.

"I will find you, Rahma," he whispered, his voice full of determination. "I promise."

REMEMBERING GRANDFATHER's WORDS

Yusuf's legs ached, his heart felt like a heavy stone, and tears streamed down his face. He had searched every inch of the meadow, but Rahma was gone. Exhausted and heartbroken, he collapsed under a big oak tree, seeking comfort in its cool shade.

He looked up at the bright blue sky, dotted with fluffy white clouds. It seemed so peaceful, so carefree. "Oh, Allah," he cried out, his voice choked with sobs. "Please help me find Rahma. I don't know what I'll do without her."

As he sat there, feeling utterly alone, he remembered something his grandfather had once told him. His grandfather, a kind, wise man, had taught him many things about life and faith.

"Yusuf, my dear," his grandfather had said, "whenever you are struggling or feeling bad about your mistakes, remember the power of Istighfar. Asking for Allah's forgiveness opens doors to His guidance and mercy. It is like a key that unlocks solutions to our problems and brings peace to our hearts. The Messenger of Allah (P.B.U.H) said, 'Whoever increases his prayers for forgiveness, Allah will grant him relief from every worry, a way out from every hardship, and provide for him in ways he does not expect.' [Musnad Aḥmad, 2234]"

At the time, Yusuf hadn't really understood what his grandfather meant. But now, as he sat under the oak tree, his heart heavy with guilt and worry, those words came back to him like a soothing melody. A tiny spark of hope flickered inside him.

Istighfar, he thought. *Seeking forgiveness.*

He knew what he had to do.

With newfound determination, Yusuf stood up and walked to a nearby stream. The water gurgled softly as he performed the wudu, washing his face, hands, and feet. It was as if he was washing away his worries and mistakes, too.

He found a quiet spot under a graceful willow tree and knelt on the soft grass. Closing his eyes, he began to pray, his heart full of hope and remorse.

"Oh Allah, the Most Merciful, the Most Forgiving," he whispered. "I have not been careful. I have failed to protect Rahma. Please, forgive me."

He poured out his heart to Allah, confessing his mistakes and asking for forgiveness. He remembered the stories his grandfather had told him about the Prophet Muhammad, peace be upon him, and how he always encouraged his followers to seek forgiveness. He recalled the verse from the Holy Quran:

"But whoever repents after their wrongdoing and mends their ways, Allah will surely turn to them in forgiveness. Indeed, Allah is All-Forgiving, Most Merciful."

[Surah Al-Ma'idah, 5:39]

As Yusuf prayed, he could feel a soothing calmness enveloping him. The heavy weight of guilt in his chest seemed to ease, replaced by a glimmer of hope. He knew in his heart that Allah (S.W.T) was listening to every word, understanding his deepest fears.

He thought about the stories he had heard of miracles that happened through prayer. He thought of Prophet Yunus, who was swallowed by a giant whale but was saved by Allah's mercy after he prayed for forgiveness. He thought of Prophet Ayyub, who suffered greatly but never lost faith in Allah, and in the end, Allah rewarded him with healing and blessings.

"Say, 'O Prophet, that Allah says,' "O My servants who have exceeded the limits against their souls! Do not lose hope in Allah's mercy, for Allah certainly forgives all sins. He is indeed the All-Forgiving, Most Merciful."

[Surah Az-Zumar, 39:53]

Yusuf's heart filled with a new sense of certainty. Allah Almighty could do anything, even bring Rahma back to him safe and sound! He just had to trust in Allah's plan.

"Oh Allah," he whispered, "please guide me to Rahma. Please keep her safe and lead me to where she is. I trust in Your mercy and Your wisdom."

When he finished praying, he felt inner peace, a feeling he hadn't felt since Rahma had gone missing. The despair that had threatened to swallow him was replaced by a spark of hope. Allah had heard his prayer. He *knew* it.

As the sun began to set, Yusuf gathered his flock and led them back to the barn. He knew he couldn't rest until he found Rahma, but he didn't feel alone anymore. He had Allah by his side, guiding him, and giving him strength.

With newfound determination, Yusuf set off once more, his voice echoing across the meadow.

"Rahma!" he called out. "Rahma, where are you?"

SEEKING HELP FROM FELLOW SHEPHERDS

Darkness fell, blanketing the land in shadows, but Yusuf wouldn't stop searching. He walked for hours, his eyes scanning every shadow, every rock, every hiding place, desperate for a glimpse of his beloved Rahma. His throat was hoarse from calling her name, but he refused to give up. He had made a promise, and he would keep it.

As he walked, he noticed a group of shepherds gathered around a crackling fire, their faces lit by the dancing flames. Feeling both shy and hopeful, he approached them.

"As-salamu alaykum," Yusuf greeted them politely.

"Wa alaykum assalam," the shepherds replied warmly.

"My name is Yusuf," he said, his voice tight with worry. "I've lost one of my sheep... a little lamb named 'Rahma'. Have any of you seen her?"

The shepherds exchanged concerned looks. They understood how much each sheep meant to a shepherd; they were like family.

"We haven't seen your lamb, young Yusuf," said an older shepherd, his brow furrowed with concern. "But tell us what she looks like, and we'll keep an eye out for her."

Yusuf described Rahma in detail: her soft brown eyes, her fluffy white wool, the tinkling bell around her neck. The shepherds listened carefully, nodding and offering words of comfort.

"Don't you worry, Yusuf," said one shepherd, a woman with eyes full of kindness and a soft, gentle smile. "Allah is with us. We'll all pray for Rahma's safe return."

As the shepherds sat around the crackling fire, sharing stories and sipping warm tea, they could feel the sadness radiating from young Yusuf. They wanted to offer him comfort and hope, so they began to share their own experiences of how seeking forgiveness from Allah had helped them overcome challenges in their lives.

The older shepherd, his face weathered by years spent under the sun and wind, spoke first.

"Years ago," he said, his voice raspy but kind, "I lost my entire flock in a terrible storm. I was heartbroken. I felt like I had failed as a shepherd." He paused, gazing thoughtfully into the flames. "But then, I remembered the power of Istighfar. I prayed to Allah, asking for His forgiveness and guidance. And you know what? The very next day, I found my entire flock! safe and sound, grazing peacefully in a hidden valley. It was a miracle!"

The shepherd woman with the kind eyes nodded in agreement. "I once had a sheep that became very ill," she said, her voice gentle. "I tried everything to heal her, but nothing worked. I was so worried I was going to lose her. But then, I turned to Allah, The Most Merciful, in prayer, asking for His forgiveness and mercy. And Alhamdulillah, my sheep made a full recovery! It was as if Allah had breathed new life into her!"

One by one, the other shepherds shared their stories, each one a testament to the power of Istighfar, of asking for Allah's forgiveness, and trusting in His boundless mercy. They spoke of financial struggles, family problems, times of fear and uncertainty... and how, in those difficult moments, turning to Allah (S.W.T) had brought them peace, guidance, and unexpected blessings.

"And whoever is mindful of Allah, He will make a way out for them, and provide for them from sources they could never imagine. And whoever puts their trust in Allah, then He 'alone' is sufficient for them. Certainly Allah achieves His Will. Allah has already set a destiny for everything."

[Surah At-Talaq, 65:2-3]

Yusuf listened intently to their stories, his heart filling with hope. He wasn't alone! Everyone faced challenges, but the shepherds reminded him that those who turned to Allah always found solace and guidance.

The older shepherd placed a hand on Yusuf's shoulder, his eyes twinkling in the firelight. "Remember, Yusuf," he said, his voice kind, "Allah is closer to us than our jugular vein. He knows our every thought and feeling. He hears our prayers, and He answers them— though sometimes in ways we don't expect."

He then recited a verse from the Holy Quran:

"Indeed, 'it is' We 'Who' created humankind and 'fully' know what their souls whisper to them, and We are closer to them than 'their' jugular vein."

[Surah Qaf, 50:16]

A feeling of warmth spread through Yusuf as he listened. He had been so focused on his own guilt and worry that he had forgotten to have faith. Allah (S.W.T) was with him, always. Hope was never lost.

REUNITED & BEING GRATEFUL

A new day dawned, and Yusuf set off again, this time with a heart full of trust in Allah. He went beyond the familiar meadows, venturing deeper into the countryside than he'd ever been before. He walked through fields bursting with colorful wildflowers, their sweet fragrance filling the air. He crossed sparkling streams, the cool water soothing his tired feet. He climbed hills, the wind whispering encouragement in his ears.

As he walked, he started to notice small things he hadn't seen before. He came across a patch of flattened grass as if a small animal had been resting there. The grass was still damp, meaning the animal had been there recently. Could it be Rahma?

Hope blossomed in his chest. He bent down and examined the ground more closely. Sure enough, he found a few strands of white wool caught on a thorny bush, just like Rahma's wool!

"Oh, Allah, please guide me," he whispered, his heart pounding with anticipation.

He continued walking, his senses alert. He listened for any sound, any movement that might lead him to Rahma. And then he heard it—a faint, familiar bleating sound in the distance.

His heart leaped! That was Rahma! He was sure of it!

He ran towards the sound, his heart pounding with every step. The bleating grew louder, leading him towards a dense thicket of trees. As he pushed through the branches, he spotted something white caught on a low-hanging branch.

It was a feather, soft and downy, just like the feathers that covered Rahma's fluffy body.

He felt an overwhelming sense of relief, joy, and gratitude. These were more than just coincidences, he realized. These were signs from Allah (S.W.T), guiding him to Rahma!

He remembered the verse from the Holy Quran:

"When My servants ask you 'O Prophet' about Me: I am truly near. I respond to one's prayer when they call upon Me. So let them respond 'with obedience' to Me and believe in Me, perhaps they will be guided 'to the Right Way'."

[Al-Baqarah, 2:186]

Yusuf had placed his trust in Allah, and now, Allah, the Trustworthy, was showing him the way, leading him to his beloved lamb.

With renewed determination, Yusuf plunged into the thicket. Rahma was close! He could feel it!

The forest grew darker and thicker. The air was heavy with the scent of damp earth. Yusuf had to duck under branches and climb over fallen logs. Thorns snagged at his clothes, and mud splattered his legs, but he didn't stop. He had come too far to give up now.

And then, at last, he saw her.

Rahma was trapped! Thorny bushes surrounded her, their sharp barbs holding her prisoner. She looked scared and helpless.

"Rahma!" Yusuf cried out, joy and relief flooding through him.

Rahma's head shot up, her eyes widening when she saw Yusuf. She bleated happily and tried to run to him, but the thorns held her fast.

Yusuf rushed to her side and carefully pushed the thorny branches aside, ignoring the scratches and pricks. Finally, he reached Rahma and gently stroked her soft wool. She was trembling!

"It's okay, Rahma," he whispered, trying to soothe her. "I'm here. I'm going to get you out."

Carefully, gently, he untangled her wool from the thorns, freeing her from her prickly prison. Rahma bleated softly and nuzzled against his leg, looking for comfort.

"Don't worry," he soothed, stroking her wool. "I'm here now."

He looked her over carefully, checking for injuries. Luckily, she seemed fine, just a little shaken up.

Once he was sure Rahma was safe and sound, Yusuf knelt on the soft grass and raised his hands in prayer.

"Oh Allah, the Most Gracious, the Most Merciful," he said, his voice thick with emotion. "Thank you for helping me find Rahma. Thank you for protecting her. Thank you for answering my prayers."

Tears of relief and joy streamed down his face. He had never felt so close to Allah, so grateful for His blessings. He realized that losing Rahma and finding her, had been a journey of faith. He had learned the true meaning of Istighfar, of seeking forgiveness and trusting in Allah's guidance.

He had learned, too, the importance of never giving up hope. He had faced challenges and moments of doubt, but he had kept his faith in Allah (S.W.T). And Allah had rewarded him beyond his wildest dreams.

"Surely in the remembrance of Allah do hearts find comfort."

[Surah Ar-Ra'd, 13:28]

Yusuf stood up, a new sense of peace and purpose filling him. Gently, he led Rahma out of the thicket, back towards the meadow.

When they reached the barn, the other sheep bleated in welcome, nuzzling and nudging Rahma with affection. Yusuf watched them, a wide smile spreading across his face. His heart felt full to bursting.

He looked up at the sky, a vibrant blue now, dotted with fluffy white clouds. The sun shone brightly, and it felt like the whole world was celebrating with him.

He knew there would be more challenges in life, and more obstacles to overcome. But now, he felt ready to face them. He had Allah Al-Mighty by his side, guiding him, giving him strength, and that was all that mattered.

He had found more than just his lost lamb; he had rediscovered his faith and deepened his connection with Allah (S.W.T). And that, he knew, was a treasure more valuable than anything else in the world.

The Messenger of Allah (P.B.U.H) said:

"If you all depend on Allah with due reliance, He would certainly give you provision as He gives it to birds who go forth hungry in the morning and return with [a] full belly at dusk." [Sunan al-Tirmidhi, 2344]

THE MANY COLORS OF RAMADAN

An Islamic Story on Learning the Diversity in Islam

RAMADAN JOY & A SEED OF DOUBT

The marketplace buzzed with excitement. Ramadan had arrived! The streets were a kaleidoscope of colors and festive cheer. Twinkling lights decorated the shops, casting a warm glow on the happy faces of people preparing for the holy month.

Amina skipped through the bustling crowd, her best friend, Kareem, by her side. His smile was as bright as the crescent moon that announced the start of Ramadan. They gazed in awe at the colorful lanterns strung between rooftops, the beautiful tapestries hanging on the walls, and breathed in the delicious aromas wafting from the food stalls.

"Ramadan is finally here!" Amina exclaimed, her voice bubbling with joy. "I love everything about it; the special prayers, the yummy food, and spending time with family."

"Me too!" Kareem agreed, his eyes sparkling. "It's a time to think about our blessings, be kind to others, and grow closer to Allah."

They passed a stall piled high with plump, juicy dates.

"Dates are the best part of breaking the fast," Kareem declared. "They're so sweet and delicious, especially after a long day of fasting."

Amina giggled. "I love dates, too! But my favorite part is praying with my family at night. It feels so peaceful and calm."

Later that evening, Amina and her family gathered in their living room for the Taraweeh prayers, a special prayer performed every night during Ramadan. They spread out their prayer rugs and began to recite verses from the Quran, their voices blending in a peaceful harmony.

Amina's heart felt full. She loved this special time, a time for her family to come together and strengthen their faith.

After the prayers, Amina peeked out her window. She could see Kareem and his family on their balcony across the street. They were gathered around a table, laughing and sharing a plate of dates.

Amina frowned. "Why aren't they praying Taraweeh?" she wondered.

A feeling of doubt crept into her heart. She had always thought that praying Taraweeh was a really important part of Ramadan. Seeing Kareem's family enjoying their evening instead of praying made her question whether they were taking Ramadan seriously.

"Maybe they're just tired," she thought, trying to come up with an explanation. But a tiny seed of doubt had been planted in her mind, and it wouldn't go away.

Amina tossed and turned in bed that night, unable to sleep. Her mind was racing with confusion. She valued her friendship with Kareem and respected his family, but she couldn't understand why they weren't following what she believed to be an important Ramadan tradition.

I have to talk to Kareem, she decided. *He'll be able to explain.* She knew that talking things out was always the best way to clear up misunderstandings and make their friendship even stronger.

OBLIGATIONS & ENHANCEMENTS

The next morning, Amina hurried to the park, eager to talk to Kareem. She found him playing with his little sister.

"Kareem, can I talk to you about something?" Amina asked, her voice a little hesitant.

Kareem could tell she was serious, so he nodded. "Of course, Amina. What's up?"

Amina took a deep breath and told him what she had seen the night before. "I noticed that your family wasn't praying Taraweeh after you broke your fast," she said. "I thought it was a really important part of Ramadan, and I was wondering why you weren't doing it."

Kareem listened patiently, his expression kind and understanding. "Amina, I'm glad you came to talk to me about this," he said. "In Islam, we have things we *must* do and things that are good to do *if we can.*

The things we *must* do are called obligations, like praying five times a day, fasting during Ramadan, and giving Zakat."

"Then there are things called enhancements," he continued. "These are extra practices that help us grow closer to Allah (S.W.T), like praying Taraweeh or reading more Quran. We are encouraged to do these things, but we won't be punished if we don't."

Amina's eyes widened. "I didn't know that!" she exclaimed. "I thought we had to do *everything*, or else we wouldn't be good Muslims during Ramadan."

Kareem smiled gently. "The Quran teaches us to focus on our obligations first, and then do the extra things if we are able to," he explained. "For example, my little sister is still learning how to pray, so my family is making sure she understands the five daily prayers before we introduce any extra ones."

He shared a saying of Prophet Muhammad (P.B.U.H) about it. The Prophet (P.B.U.H) was asked, "What deeds are loved most by Allah?" He said, "The most regular constant deeds even though they may be few." He added, "Don't take upon yourselves, except the deeds which are within your ability." *[Reference: Sahih Al-Bukhari, 6465]*

Amina listened carefully, her mind spinning. She always wanted to please Allah and do as much as possible. But maybe, she realized, she'd been focusing too much on how *much* she was doing, instead of understanding *why* she was doing it.

"So, it's okay if we don't do *all* the extra things?" she asked, still a little unsure.

"Of course," Kareem reassured her. "The most important thing is to have a sincere heart and good intentions. Allah knows what's in our hearts, and He appreciates all our efforts, big or small."

Amina was relieved. She realized she'd been wrong to judge Kareem's family. There were different ways to practice and celebrate Ramadan!

"Thank you for explaining this to me, Kareem," she said, a grateful smile spreading across her face. "I understand now. It's not about doing everything perfectly; it's about trying our best and having a sincere heart."

Kareem smiled back. "And remember, Amina, we are all on a journey of faith. We learn and grow together. Let's support each other and celebrate the beautiful diversity in our religion."

Amina nodded, her heart full of a new understanding. It was like a beautiful garden, the Garden of Faith, where everyone could grow and bloom in their own special way.

DIFFERENT FLOWERS, SAME GARDEN

Kareem's explanation about Islamic practices had really opened Amina's eyes. She felt a bit ashamed that she had judged his family so quickly.

I need to talk to Mom and Dad about this, she thought. They were always so wise and understanding.

That evening, after enjoying a delicious meal of lentil soup and dates to break their fast, Amina sat down with her parents in the living room.

"Mama, Papa," she began, fiddling with her fingers, "I was talking to Kareem today about Ramadan prayers, and he told me something I didn't know."

She told her parents about seeing Kareem's family, her confusion about them not praying Taraweeh, and what Kareem had explained about obligations and enhancements in Islam.

"I feel bad for judging them," she admitted. "I want to understand more about the different ways people practice our faith."

Amina's parents listened patiently, their faces full of love and understanding.

"Amina, it's wonderful that you're asking questions and thinking about your actions," her mother said gently. "Just like a garden needs strong roots to support its beautiful flowers, our faith needs a strong foundation of essential practices before we can add extra ones."

"The Quran teaches us that Allah doesn't want us to struggle," her father added. "We should focus on fulfilling our obligations with sincerity and devotion. As our faith grows stronger, we can gradually add other practices that will enrich our spiritual journey."

He shared a verse from the Quran:

"Allah intends ease for you, not hardship,"

[Surah Al-Baqarah, 2:185]

"Remember, Amina," her mother continued, "everyone's journey of faith is different. Just like every flower in a garden blooms at its own pace and has its unique beauty, each person connects with Allah in their own way."

She reminded Amina how important it was to respect other people's choices and not to judge them. "The Prophet Muhammad, peace be upon him, taught us to be kind and compassionate to one another. He said, 'None of you truly believes until he loves for his brother what he loves for himself.' We should focus on our actions and not compare ourselves to others."

The Prophet Muhammad (P.B. U.H):

"The believers are like one body in their mutual love, mercy, and compassion. If one part of the body suffers, the whole body feels the pain." [Sahih al-Bukhari, 6011]

Amina thought carefully about her mother's words. She realized that she had judged Kareem's family without understanding their situation.

"I feel bad for judging them," Amina admitted, her voice full of regret. "I should have talked to Kareem first instead of thinking I knew better."

Her father smiled reassuringly. "It's okay, Amina. Everyone makes mistakes. The important thing is that you realized your mistake, learned from it, and will try to do better next time."

"I want to apologize to Kareem and his family," Amina said, determined to make things right. "I want them to know that I respect the way they practice Islam."

Her parents' faces glowed with pride.

"That's a wonderful idea, Amina," her mother said. "Asking for forgiveness and making things right is a sign that you're growing and maturing."

Amina had learned an important lesson that day. She learned that it was always best to ask for guidance from people she trusted, like her parents, to think carefully about her actions, and to be open to learning new things. She also learned how important it was to respect other people's choices and to appreciate that everyone practices their faith in their own way.

A HEARTFELT APOLOGY | SHARING TRADITIONS

The next afternoon, Amina's heart thumped like a drum as she walked toward Kareem and his family in the park. She had spent the whole morning thinking about what she wanted to say and practicing her apology.

She found Kareem and his little sister playing on the swings.

"Kareem, can I talk to you and your family for a minute?" she asked, her voice sincere.

Kareem looked up, a gentle smile on his face. "Of course, Amina," he said. "What's up?"

Amina felt her cheeks grow warm. "I wanted to apologize for what I said yesterday about the Taraweeh prayers," she confessed. "I was wrong to judge your family, and I understand now that there are different ways to celebrate Ramadan."

Kareem's smile widened and his eyes twinkled. "Thank you for apologizing, Amina," he said kindly. "We appreciate it."

Kareem's mom and dad, who had been sitting on a nearby bench, walked over with warm smiles on their faces.

"Amina, we are so proud of you for admitting your mistake and for wanting to understand," Kareem's mom said, her voice full of warmth.

"Ramadan is a time for reflection and growth, and it sounds like you have learned a valuable lesson."

Amina felt a wave of comfort. Kareem and his family weren't angry with her at all! They accepted her apology with open arms.

"We understand that everyone practices their faith in their own way," Kareem's father said. "The beauty of Islam is in its diversity. All the different cultures and traditions make our religion even richer."

He told Amina a story about growing up in Morocco, where his family would gather in the evenings during Ramadan to listen to stories of Prophets, recite Naats of Prophet Muhammad (P.B.U.H), and learn the history of Islam.

"It was a way for us to connect with our heritage and learn more about our faith," he explained. "We didn't pray Taraweeh every night, but we found other ways to make Ramadan special."

"In my family," Kareem's mother added, "we have a tradition of cooking special meals for people in need during Ramadan. It's our way of sharing our blessings and spreading kindness."

Amina listened intently as Kareem and his parents shared their Ramadan traditions. She realized that Ramadan wasn't about following a strict set of rules; it was about the feelings in your heart and the reasons behind your actions.

"I used to think that *my* way of celebrating Ramadan was the *only* right way," Amina admitted. "But now I see that there are so many beautiful ways to celebrate and connect with Allah."

Kareem nodded. "It's like a garden," he said, his eyes sparkling. "Every flower is different... different colors, different shapes, different smells... but they all make the garden beautiful."

Amina smiled. She understood exactly what he meant. "The Garden of Faith," she whispered, a feeling of awe washing over her.

From that day on, Amina and Kareem's friendship grew even stronger, built on a foundation of respect, understanding, and their shared faith. They continued to learn from each other, appreciating the many ways people celebrate Islamic traditions and focusing on the essential principles that united them as Muslims.

THE GARDEN OF FAITH BLOOMS

Excitement filled the air as the last day of Ramadan came to a close. The crescent moon, now full and bright, signaled the arrival of Eid-ul-Fitr, the festival of breaking the fast. Joy and gratitude rippled through the community as families prepared to celebrate the end of the holy month.

Amina woke up early on Eid morning, her heart brimming with excitement. She helped her mother prepare delicious treats: sheer khurma, a sweet vermicelli pudding, and colorful cookies decorated with intricate patterns. The aroma of spices and sweetness filled their home, creating a festive atmosphere.

Later that morning, Amina and her family dressed in their finest clothes. Amina wore a bright, colorful dress with sparkling jewelry, and her brother wore a crisp, new kurta. They joined the crowds of people heading towards the mosque for the special Eid prayer.

The mosque overflowed with families, friends, and neighbors, everyone dressed in their best clothes. A feeling of unity and joy filled the air as they stood shoulder-to-shoulder, offering prayers of thanks to Allah (S.W.T).

Ibn Abbas (r.a) narrated that the Messenger of Allah (P.B.U.H) said:

"When the day of Eid al-Fitr [begins], the angels descend on earth, where they take their positions at access points of roads, calling out with a voice that is heard by the whole creation of Allah, except men and Jin, 'O Ummah of Muhammad (saw)! Come out to your most Noble and Gracious Lord, who grants much, and pardons the major sins.'

When they (the Ummah) proceed to their places of prayer, Allah, Exalted is He, says to His angels, 'O My angels! What is the reward of a worker when he has done his work?'

So they (the angels) say, 'Our Lord and Our Master! To receive his reward [for the work, in full].'

So He (S.W.T) says, 'I call you to witness that, for their fasts [during Ramadan], and for their standing in prayer at night, I have made their reward My Pleasure, and my Forgiveness. Depart [from here], you are forgiven.'" [Lataif al-Ma'arif]

After the prayer, Amina spotted Kareem and his family in the crowd. Their faces were glowing with happiness, their eyes sparkling with excitement. Amina hurried over to them, a huge smile on her face.

"Eid Mubarak!" she exclaimed, hugging Kareem and his sister.

"Eid Mubarak, Amina!" they replied, hugging her back.

Amina's family and Kareem's family exchanged warm greetings and hugs. They decided to celebrate Eid together, sharing a delicious meal and enjoying each other's company.

As they gathered around a table laden with delicious food, Amina thought about everything she had learned during Ramadan. She had learned so much about the different ways people practice Islam, about the importance of understanding and acceptance, and what it really means to have faith.

She looked at Kareem and his family with a newfound appreciation. They had taught her so much about prioritizing, about having good intentions, and about respecting the many ways people practice their faith.

Amina reached into her bag and pulled out a box of dates. "I brought these for you," she said, offering the box to Kareem and his family with a shy smile. "I know how much you like them."

Kareem's eyes lit up, and his family beamed with delight. "Thank you, Amina!" he exclaimed. "That's so thoughtful of you."

They shared the sweet dates, a symbol of the sweetness of their understanding and friendship. Amina's heart swelled with gratitude. She felt a deep connection not just with Kareem and his family, but with the entire Muslim community.

They spent the rest of the day celebrating Eid together. They shared stories and laughter, played games, exchanged gifts, and visited other friends and family. The spirit of Eid filled the air, a reminder of the importance of gratitude, compassion, and unity.

As the day drew to a close, and the stars twinkled in the night sky, Amina and Kareem thought about everything they had learned during Ramadan. They had grown closer to Allah, learned more about their faith, and their friendship was stronger than ever.

"Ramadan may be over," Kareem said, "but our journey of faith continues."

Amina nodded. "And we'll keep walking that path together," she agreed.

They were excited to keep learning and growing in their faith, to support each other, and to celebrate the many beautiful ways people practice Islam. Together, they would help the Garden of Faith bloom, both in their hearts and in their community.

NO TWO FLOWERS ARE THE SAME

An Islamic Story on Appreciating the Differences

UNCLE KHALIL & HIS BEAUTIFUL GARDEN

The warm sun peeked through the curtains, tickling Halima awake. She stretched like a lazy cat and hopped out of bed. Today was a special day—she was going to visit Uncle Khalil! He had the most wonderful garden in the whole neighborhood, filled with colorful flowers, buzzing bees, and juicy fruits.

Halima quickly got dressed and rushed downstairs, where her brother Aasim was already waiting, bouncing with excitement. Their friend Yasmin soon arrived, her eyes sparkling with anticipation.

"Are we ready to see Uncle Khalil's magical garden?" asked Halima.

"Yes!" shouted Aasim and Yasmin together, and they skipped out the door, holding hands.

Uncle Khalil's garden was a paradise. Butterflies fluttered among the flowers, birds sang sweet songs, and the air smelled of sunshine and fresh earth. Uncle Khalil, with his kind eyes and gentle smile, greeted them with a warm hug.

"Welcome, my little sprouts!" he chuckled. "Today, we are going to discover something magical."

He led them to a shady spot under a large tree and opened a basket overflowing with little packets. Each packet held something special—seeds! There were sunflower seeds, round and plump; tiny black poppy seeds; long, thin carrot seeds; and even prickly cactus seeds.

"Wow!" gasped Yasmin. "So many different seeds!"

"Each of these seeds," Uncle Khalil explained, "holds a secret inside. It's like a tiny treasure waiting to grow into something beautiful."

He picked up a sunflower seed and held it gently between his fingers. "This seed, for example, has the secret of a tall, bright sunflower inside. It dreams of reaching for the sun and showing off its golden petals."

Aasim picked up a cactus seed. "And this one?" he asked, turning the spiky seed over in his palm.

"Ah, the cactus seed," Uncle Khalil said with a smile. "It holds the secret of a strong, sturdy plant that can survive even in the driest desert. It may not have soft petals like a flower, but it has a unique beauty of its own."

Halima picked a small, brown seed that looked quite ordinary. "What about this one, Uncle Khalil?"

"That, my dear," he said, his eyes twinkling, "is a rose seed. Inside it sleeps the secret of a beautiful rose, with soft petals and a sweet fragrance. But it takes time and patience for the rose to bloom."

The children were fascinated. They carefully examined each seed, imagining the plants hidden within.

"Just like these seeds," Uncle Khalil continued, "each one of you has a secret inside; your own special way of growing and blooming. Some of you might be like sunflowers, bright and cheerful. Others might be like cactus, strong and independent. And some might be like roses, taking time to blossom but spreading beauty and kindness wherever they go."

Halima, Aasim, and Yasmin looked at each other, wondering what their own secret might be.

"Come," Uncle Khalil said, leading them toward the garden beds. "Let's plant these seeds and watch them grow. We can learn a lot about ourselves by watching how our plants change and blossom."

The children carefully planted their chosen seeds in the soft earth in the pot. They watered them gently and promised to take good care of them.

As they walked away from the garden, hand in hand with Uncle Khalil, they couldn't wait to see what secrets their seeds would reveal.

GROWING IN DIFFERENT WAYS

Every day after school, Halima, Aasim, and Yasmin would race to Uncle Khalil's garden, hoping to catch the first glimpse of a sprout pushing through the soil. They couldn't wait to see their little seeds and how much they had grown.

Yasmin was the first to see a change in her sunflower seed. One sunny morning, she noticed a tiny green shoot emerging from the earth. "Look!" she cried, pointing excitedly. "My sunflower is growing!"

The little shoot stretched towards the sun, growing taller each day. Soon, it unfurled its first leaves, reaching out like tiny green hands. Yasmin felt a burst of pride. Her sunflower was the fastest-growing plant of them all!

Aasim's cactus seed took its time. Days turned into weeks, and still, there was no sign of life. He started to worry. Maybe he wasn't watering it enough, or perhaps it wasn't getting enough sunlight.

One day, as he knelt beside his pot, feeling a little discouraged, he noticed something. A tiny bump had appeared, pushing its way through the soil. It wasn't a tall shoot like Yasmin's sunflower, but a small, round ball with tiny prickles. It was his cactus, finally starting to grow!

Halima's rose seed seemed to be taking the longest. While Yasmin's sunflower was already tall and Aasim's cactus was showing its prickly personality, her pot remained quiet.

"Don't worry, Halima," Uncle Khalil comforted her. "Remember, the rose takes its time to bloom. It's busy growing strong roots underground, preparing for the day it will share its beautiful flower with the world. Our Prophet Muhammad (P.B.U.H) said:

"Nobody can be given a blessing better and greater than patience." [Sahih Al-Bukhari, Book 24 Hadith 548].

Halima trusted Uncle Khalil. She patiently watered her rose seed and spoke kind words to it, hoping to encourage it to grow.

As the weeks went by, the children observed the unique ways their plants grew. Yasmin's sunflower shot up towards the sky, reaching for the sun with all its might. Its stem grew thick and strong, and soon, a large bud appeared at the top.

Aasim's cactus grew slowly but steadily. It developed more prickly bumps, creating a tough armor around itself. Although it wasn't as tall as the sunflower, it had a unique strength and resilience.

Halima's rose finally started to sprout. A tiny green shoot emerged from the soil, slowly unfurling its delicate leaves. It was much smaller than the sunflower and not as prickly as the cactus, but it had a gentle beauty that was all its own.

The children learned that just like their plants, everyone grows and develops differently. Some, like Yasmin's sunflower, might achieve things quickly and stand out from the crowd. Others, like

Aasim's cactus, might grow slowly but possess a hidden strength. And some, like Halima's rose, might take their time to bloom but eventually share their unique beauty with the world.

Every visit to Uncle Khalil's garden was a lesson in patience, understanding, and appreciation for the diverse ways in which things grow and flourish. They learned that each plant, like each person, had its unique way of being, and that was something to celebrate.

THE COMPARISON TRAP

Yasmin's sunflower was the star of the garden. It stood tall and proud, towering over the other plants. Its bright yellow petals unfurled like a king's crown, facing the sun with confidence. Yasmin couldn't help but feel a little boastful.

"Look at my sunflower!" she'd exclaim to Aasim and Halima. "It's the tallest and the most beautiful!" She puffed out her chest and held her head high, feeling like the sunflower's success was her own.

Aasim, on the other hand, felt a pang of sadness whenever he saw Yasmin's sunflower. His little cactus, though strong and healthy, seemed so small and insignificant in comparison. Its prickly exterior hid a growing feeling of meagerness.

"My cactus is just a prickly ball," he mumbled to himself one day. "It's not as impressive as Yasmin's sunflower. Nobody will ever want to look at it." He felt a little jealous of Yasmin and wished his plant was more like hers.

Halima watched her rose bush with a worried frown. While it had grown taller and sprouted several leaves, there was still no sign of a flower bud. She started to compare her rose to the other roses she had seen in books and pictures; roses with large, fragrant blooms in vibrant colors.

"My rose is taking too long," she thought with a sigh. "What if it never blooms? What if it's not as beautiful as the other roses?" She started to doubt her little plant and its ability to blossom.

One afternoon, as the children gathered in Uncle Khalil's garden, the comparison trap began to tighten its grip. Yasmin, unable to contain her pride, started bragging about her sunflower.

"My sunflower is the best in the whole garden!" she declared. "It's taller than all the others, and its petals are the brightest yellow!"

Aasim kicked at the dirt, feeling his cheeks grow hot with frustration. "Well, at least my cactus is strong," he muttered under his breath, but his voice lacked belief.

Halima stayed quiet, lost in her worries. She looked at her rose bush with a disappointed sigh, comparing its small size and lack of blooms to the vibrant flowers in Uncle Khalil's garden.

Uncle Khalil noticed the change in the children's behavior. He saw the pride in Yasmin's eyes, the discouragement in Aasim's posture, and the worry etched on Halima's face. He knew he needed to help them escape the comparison trap before it took away their joy and gratitude.

He gathered the children around him and said, "My dear little gardeners, I see that you are comparing your plants to each other. But remember, each seed has its unique journey, just like each one of you. And never look down upon each other. Always remember this saying of our Holy Prophet (P.BU.H):

'Do not envy each other, do not outbid each other, do not hate each other, do not turn away from each other, and do not outsell each other. Rather, be servants of Allah as brothers. The Muslim is the brother of another Muslim. He does not wrong him, nor humiliate him, nor look down upon him. Righteousness is here,' and he pointed to his chest three times. The Prophet (P.B.U.H) said, 'It is enough evil for a man to look down upon his Muslim brother. The entirety of the Muslim is sacred to another Muslim: his life, his wealth, and his reputation.'" [Sahih Muslim, 2564]

The children looked at him, their eyes filled with embarrassment.

"Yasmin," Uncle Khalil said gently, "your sunflower is indeed tall and beautiful. But its purpose isn't to be better than any other plant. Its purpose is to reach for the sun, to spread its seeds, and to bring joy with its bright colors."

Yasmin looked down at her feet, realizing that she had been so focused on her sunflower being the best, that she had forgotten to appreciate its own unique qualities.

Uncle Khalil turned to Aasim. "Aasim, your cactus may not be as tall or showy as the sunflower, but it has a strength that is all its own. It can survive harsh conditions and protect itself with its prickly armor. It teaches us about resilience and perseverance."

Aasim looked at his cactus with newfound respect. He realized that its strength and ability to thrive in difficult conditions were qualities to be admired, not looked down upon.

Finally, Uncle Khalil addressed Halima. "Halima, your rose may take time to bloom, but that doesn't mean it's not beautiful. It's busy growing strong roots and preparing to share its fragrance and delicate petals with the world. It teaches us about patience and the beauty of waiting for the right moment."

Halima felt a warmth spread through her heart. She understood that her rose was on its unique journey, and she needed to trust the process and appreciate its progress, however slow it might seem.

Uncle Khalil smiled at the children. "Remember," he said, "Allah has created each one of us with a special purpose and unique qualities. Comparing ourselves to others only takes away from the joy of discovering our strengths and appreciating the gifts we have been given."

He looked towards the sky and added, "Just like the sun, the moon, and the stars, each one of us shines in our own way."

"Don't compare yourself to others," he said gently. "Focus on growing and learning, and appreciate all the differences around you. Remember, in a garden, it's not about one flower being better than another. It's about how all the different plants come together to create something beautiful and harmonious. That's what makes a garden special, just like how your different personalities and talents make our world so wonderful."

The children took Uncle Khalil's words to heart. They realized that they had fallen into the comparison trap, focusing on what they lacked instead of appreciating what they had.

Yasmin decided to celebrate her sunflower's height and brightness without boasting. Aasim learned to admire his cactus's strength and resilience. And Halima patiently waited for her rose to bloom, trusting that it would be beautiful in its own time.

As the sun dipped below the horizon, the children went home feeling grateful and enlightened. They had learned a valuable lesson: true happiness doesn't come from comparing yourself to others. It comes from embracing your unique qualities and appreciating the blessings that Allah, the Most Gracious, the Most Merciful, has given you.

EMBRACING OUR UNIQUE QUALITIES
& CELEBRATING DIVERSITY

The wise words of Uncle Khalil continued to resonate in their thoughts.

Yasmin thought about how she had boasted about her sunflower, wanting it to be the best and tallest. She realized that her pride had blinded her to the beauty of the other plants and the unique qualities they possessed.

Aasim reflected on his feelings of inadequacy about his cactus. He understood now that strength and resilience were just as important as height and showy petals. He felt a newfound appreciation for his prickly little plant and its ability to thrive in harsh conditions.

Halima's heart softened as she thought about her rose bush. She had been so focused on when it would bloom and how it would compare to other roses that she had forgotten to appreciate its delicate leaves and the promise of its sweet fragrance.

They knew they had hurt each other with their comparisons and wanted to make things right.

"Aasim, I'm sorry I bragged about my sunflower," Yasmin said sincerely. "Your cactus is amazing, and I shouldn't have made you feel bad."

Aasim smiled. "It's okay, Yasmin. I was wrong to feel jealous. Your sunflower is beautiful, and I should have just been happy for you."

Halima looked at her friends with tears welling up in her eyes. "I'm sorry too," she said in a small voice. "I was so worried about my rose not blooming that I forgot to appreciate all the wonderful things about your plants."

Yasmin and Aasim hugged Halima tightly. They had all been caught in the comparison trap, but they were determined to do better.

The next day, they returned to Uncle Khalil's garden with a new sense of purpose. They focused on caring for their plants with love and attention, noticing their individual needs and appreciating their unique qualities.

Yasmin gently tied her sunflower to a stake, supporting its tall stem. She admired its bright yellow petals and imagined the seeds it would soon produce.

Aasim carefully removed a few weeds that had grown around his cactus, ensuring it had enough space to thrive. He marveled at its resilience and the way it stood strong against the elements.

Halima watered her rose bush and whispered words of encouragement. She noticed tiny buds forming at the tips of the branches, a promise of the beautiful blooms to come.

As they worked together, a sense of peace and harmony filled the garden. They realized that comparing themselves to others had only brought negativity and unhappiness. They understood that just as Allah (S.W.T) had created a diverse and beautiful garden with plants of all shapes, sizes, and colors, He had also created each of them with unique talents and purposes.

From that day on, Halima, Aasim, and Yasmin nurtured their plants and their friendships with love, acceptance, and gratitude, knowing that true happiness bloomed from within, just like the beautiful flowers in Uncle Khalil's garden.

BLOOMING WITH GRATITUDE

Days turned into weeks, and weeks into months. With each passing day, the children's plants continued to grow and thrive under their loving care. The once tiny seeds had transformed into strong, healthy plants, each showcasing its unique beauty and character.

Yasmin's sunflower stood tall and proud, its golden head reaching for the sky. The bright yellow petals seemed to radiate sunshine, attracting bees and butterflies with their sweet nectar. Soon, the center of the sunflower began to fill with seeds, promising a delicious harvest in the weeks to come.

Aasim's cactus had grown taller and sturdier. Its once small, prickly bumps had developed into a formidable armor, protecting it from harsh weather and hungry animals. Aasim admired its resilience and strength, knowing that it could survive even the toughest conditions.

Halima's rose bush had finally blossomed. Delicate pink petals unfurled, revealing a heart of golden stamens. The sweet fragrance of the rose filled the air, attracting hummingbirds and bringing a smile to everyone's face. Halima's patience and care had been rewarded with a breathtaking display of beauty.

One sunny afternoon, the children gathered in Uncle Khalil's garden to celebrate their plants' achievements. They admired the tall sunflower, the strong cactus, and the fragrant rose, each unique and beautiful in its way.

"Look how far we've come," said Yasmin, her eyes sparkling with joy. "Our plants have grown so much, and they're all so different!"

"Just like us," added Aasim, a wide grin on his face. "We all have our own strengths and weaknesses, but that's what makes us special."

Halima nodded in agreement. "And we've learned that comparing ourselves to others only takes away from our own happiness. We should be grateful for what we have and appreciate our unique qualities."

Uncle Khalil smiled warmly at the children. He was proud of how far they had come. They had learned valuable lessons about gratitude, self-acceptance, and the importance of celebrating differences.

"Remember," he said, "just as Allah (S.W.T) has created a diverse and beautiful world filled with plants, animals, and people of all kinds,

He has also given each of us unique talents and purposes. We must discover and nurture these gifts and use them to make the world a better place."

He placed a hand on Aasim's shoulder. "Always remember to be grateful for Allah's blessings, big and small. Be kind to yourselves and to others, and never stop learning and growing. Allah (S.W.T) says in the Quran:

"...And if you should count the favors of Allah, you could not enumerate them." [Surah Ibrahim, 14:34]

The children hugged Uncle Khalil tightly, thanking him for his wisdom and guidance. They knew they would carry his lessons with them throughout their lives.

As the children left the garden, hand in hand, they paused to look back at their plants. Each one was a symbol of their journey and a reminder of the beauty of individuality. They understood now that true happiness wasn't about comparing themselves to others, but about connecting with Allah, appreciating His blessings, and nurturing their unique qualities.

Just like their plants, each child was a unique and beautiful creation, contributing to the vibrant tapestry of life. They knew that with gratitude, self-acceptance, and a strong connection to Allah, they could flourish wherever they went, spreading kindness, joy, and beauty throughout the world.

SHAWANA'S TIME TRAVEL ADVENTURE

An Islamic Story on Journey to the Golden Age of Islam

SHAWANA's DILEMMA & THE ANTIQUES SHOP

Shawana loved gazing up at the night sky. The twinkling stars, the silvery moon, and the vastness of it all; it filled her with wonder.

"Mama," she'd ask, her eyes wide with curiosity, "how many stars are there? How far away is the moon?"

Her mama would smile and say, "Only Allah knows, my dear. But science can help us learn about them."

To Shawana, science was like magic! It explained how everything worked, from tiny ants crawling on the ground to giant planets swirling in space. She loved reading about famous scientists, doing little experiments at home, and dreaming of making her own discoveries someday.

But Shawana also loved learning about Islam. She loved going to the mosque with her family, listening to wonderful stories of the Prophets, and reading the Quran. Her faith was like a warm light inside her, guiding her to be kind, honest, and helpful.

Sometimes, Shawana felt confused. Some people told her that focusing on science and other "worldly" subjects would distract her from her religion. They said she should spend more time studying the Quran and Islamic teachings.

Shawana didn't understand. Why couldn't she love both science and Islam? Allah (S.W.T) created *everything*, so learning about His creation seemed like a way to feel *closer* to Him, not further away.

One day, Shawana came home from school feeling down. She'd aced her science test, but her aunt, who was visiting, had said, "Shawana, you're so good at science! But don't forget to focus on your religious studies, too. That's what's truly important."

Shawana went to her room and looked at her bookshelf. One half was filled with science books; colorful pictures of planets and animals. The other half held her Islamic books; beautiful calligraphy and lessons from the life of the Prophets and pious people.

She sighed. "Why do they have to be separate?" she wondered. "Why can't they be together?"

Just then, her father called out, "Shawana, get ready! We're going to the old marketplace!"

Shawana loved the old marketplace. It was like stepping back in time! Narrow alleys twisted and turned between shops bursting with colorful goods. The air was thick with the scent of spices and sweet treats. Today, Shawana and her father were on a mission to find some antique decorations for their living room.

As they made their way through the bustling marketplace, Shawana saw shopkeepers selling all sorts of things; handcrafted pottery, shimmering fabrics, beautifully painted boxes. The air buzzed with the sounds of people bargaining, laughing, and the rhythmic clang of a coppersmith hammering metal.

Suddenly, Shawana spotted a small, dusty shop tucked away in a corner. A sign above it read, "Antique Treasures". Curiosity bubbled inside her.

"Baba, can we go inside? Please?" she asked, tugging on her father's sleeve.

Her father smiled. "Of course, Shawana," he said. "Let's see what treasures we can find."

Little did Shawana know that this dusty little shop held the answer to her questions... and the beginning of an incredible adventure that would change the way she saw the world.

THE AMAZING ASTROLABE

Stepping into the antique shop was like stepping into another world. The air was thick with dust and the scent of old paper. A single ray of sunlight streamed through a small window, illuminating a jumble of curious objects: ancient lamps, chipped teacups, faded tapestries, and piles of books with yellowed pages.

Shawana's eyes darted from one treasure to the next. A tarnished silver locket shaped like a crescent moon, a wooden box carved with swirling patterns, a chipped ceramic plate painted with vibrant flowers... Each object seemed to whisper stories of forgotten times.

"Careful, Shawana," her father chuckled. "You might get lost in here!"

Suddenly, something shiny caught Shawana's eye. On a dusty shelf, nestled between a chipped vase and a worn-out book, lay a circular object made of brass. It looked like a compass mixed with a star chart, with intricate markings and moving parts.

"Baba, what's that?" Shawana asked, pointing.

Her father carefully picked it up and blew off the dust. "This, my dear, is an astrolabe," he explained. "Sailors and astronomers used it to navigate by the stars and tell time."

Shawana traced her finger along the cool metal, amazed by its intricate details. It felt strangely warm under her fingertips as if it held a secret waiting to be discovered.

"Can I hold it, Baba?" she asked eagerly.

Her father hesitated for a moment, then nodded. "Be careful, Shawana," he warned. "It's very old."

Shawana carefully took the astrolabe, turning it over in her hands. As she studied its intricate markings and dials, she felt a strange tingling sensation. The shop around her seemed to blur, and the sounds of the marketplace faded away.

She looked up, but her father was gone! And the antique shop had vanished, too! Instead, she found herself standing in a bustling marketplace that felt both familiar and strange.

The stalls were made of wood and canvas, overflowing with exotic spices, colorful fabrics, and gleaming metalwork. People wearing turbans and long robes bustled about, bargaining with shopkeepers and chatting with each other. The air was filled with tempting smells; roasting meat, sweet pastries, strong tea...

Shawana froze, clutching the astrolabe tightly. Where was she? Had she traveled back in time?

Suddenly, a boy about her age bumped into her, nearly knocking her off her feet.

"Oh, I'm so sorry!" he exclaimed, his eyes wide with concern. He had a mischievous grin and bright, curious eyes. "Are you alright?"

Shawana nodded, still feeling dazed. "I'm fine," she said. "But... where am I?"

The boy's eyebrows shot up in surprise. "You're in the marketplace, of course! Don't you know?"

Confused, Shawana shook her head. "But... it looks different. The clothes, the shops... it's like I've stepped into a history book!"

The boy laughed. "A history book? What a strange thing to say! My name is Sulaiman. What's yours?"

"Shawana," she replied, still feeling a little lost.

Sulaiman's grin widened. "Welcome to the marketplace, Shawana! Come on, let me show you around."

He grabbed her hand and pulled her through the bustling crowd, giving her a whirlwind tour of the marketplace.

SULAIMAN & THE WORLD OF NUMBERS

Sulaiman loved the marketplace more than any other place in the world. It wasn't just the colorful sights and delicious smells that fascinated him; it was the way numbers played a role in everything.

He loved watching the merchants carefully weigh spices on their scales, measuring each gram with precision. He'd listen intently as they calculated prices, adding and subtracting with ease. Even the way they arranged their goods in neat rows and stacks seemed to follow a hidden numerical order.

Sulaiman's favorite person in the marketplace was Mustafa, a wise and honest merchant. Mustafa's shop was filled with treasures from faraway lands: silks from China, spices from India, and beautiful carpets from Persia. But what fascinated Sulaiman most was how meticulously Mustafa kept track of everything.

He watched as Mustafa carefully wrote down every transaction in his leather-bound ledger, using elegant Arabic script and precise numbers. He recorded the quantity of each item sold, the price, and the name of the buyer.

One day, Sulaiman gathered his courage and asked, "Uncle Mustafa, why do you write everything down so carefully?"

Mustafa smiled warmly at Sulaiman. "Ah, young Sulaiman," he said, "keeping good records is essential for any business. It helps us remember what we have sold, what we need to order, and how much money we have earned. It also makes sure things are fair for both the buyer and the seller. We follow the teachings of the Quran, which reminds us to be honest and just in all our dealings."

He showed Sulaiman a verse from the Quran written beautifully in his ledger:

"You should not become weary to write it (your contract), whether it be small or big, for its fixed term, that is more just with Allah; more solid as evidence, and more convenient to prevent doubts among yourselves,"

[Surah Baqarah, 2:282]

Sulaiman's eyes widened. He'd heard that verse in his Quran lessons, but he'd never thought about it applying to something like buying and selling!

"Writing things down helps prevent confusion and arguments," Mustafa continued. "It also helps us learn and grow. By looking at our records, we can see which things are selling well, which aren't, and how we can improve our business."

Sulaiman nodded eagerly, his mind buzzing. Numbers weren't just symbols on a page; they were tools for fairness, organization, and learning! He started to see the marketplace in a whole new light; it was like a giant classroom where numbers came to life!

From that day on, Sulaiman practiced his numbers every chance he got. He'd use charcoal to write on scraps of parchment, adding and subtracting imaginary amounts of dates, figs, and spices. He even created his own pretend shop, arranging pebbles and shells like they were merchandise and recording imaginary sales.

***

Sulaiman, eager to share his world, introduced Shawana to the merchants and their wares. He showed her how the scales worked, how prices were calculated, and explained that the intricate patterns on the carpets were created using mathematical principles.

Shawana's eyes sparkled with fascination. A calligrapher was writing elegant verses on a scroll. A potter was shaping clay into beautiful vases. A merchant was carefully weighing spices on a brass scale. This wasn't just a marketplace; it was a place buzzing with knowledge and culture. And somehow, she had become a part of it!

She listened attentively to Sulaiman's explanations, asking questions and sharing her own observations. Sulaiman was impressed by how much she knew and how curious she was. He'd never met anyone who was so interested in numbers and how things worked!

As they walked through the marketplace, Shawana noticed that everyone seemed to be writing and calculating. Shopkeepers used ink and quills to record their transactions. Customers carefully counted their coins before making purchases. Even children were practicing their numbers on small wooden boards.

"You seem really interested in numbers, Shawana," Sulaiman observed, a smile spreading across his face.

Shawana's face lit up. "I am!" she exclaimed. "Back home, I love learning about science and how things work. It's like magic but with numbers and logic instead of spells!"

Sulaiman's eyes sparkled. "I know exactly what you mean!" he said. "I love numbers, too. Everything in the marketplace depends on them; measuring ingredients, figuring out prices, even arranging things so they look nice."

He led Shawana to his favorite stall in the whole marketplace. It was overflowing with colorful spices. Mustafa, the kind merchant, stood behind the counter.

"This is Uncle Mustafa," Sulaiman said proudly, introducing Shawana. "He's the best merchant in the whole marketplace, and he knows everything about numbers!"

Mustafa chuckled, his eyes twinkling. "Ah, young Sulaiman always exaggerates," he said. "But I do believe that numbers and keeping accurate records are important. It ensures fairness for everyone and pleases Allah (S.W.T)."

He gestured toward his ledger, a thick book filled with neat rows of numbers and elegant Arabic script. "The Quran teaches us to document our transactions and be truthful in our dealings," he explained. "Numbers help us do that."

The Prophet (P.B.U.H) said:

"The honest and trustworthy merchant will be with the
Prophets, the truthful, and the martyrs."
[Sunan al-Tirmidhi, 1209]

Shawana, who had been listening closely, suddenly felt like everything clicked into place. She'd always felt a division between her love of science and her faith, but here, in this bustling marketplace, she saw how they could be connected. Numbers weren't just for trade; they were a way to live by Islamic values of honesty and justice.

Sulaiman, noticing her thoughtful expression, added, "Uncle Mustafa says that numbers are like a language. They tell stories, help us understand the world, and even connect us to Allah's creation."

Shawana nodded, feeling a sense of wonder. "That's just like science!" she exclaimed. "It helps us understand the universe that Allah created, from tiny insects to huge galaxies!"

Mustafa smiled, his eyes twinkling. "Indeed, young Shawana," he said. "All knowledge, whether it's about numbers, stars, or the words of the Quran, is a gift from Allah. And using that knowledge for good is a way to worship Him and serve His creation."

"And to Allah (belongs) the Kingdom of the heavens and the earth; and Allah has power over all things. Verily! In the creation of the heavens and the earth, and in the alternation of night and day, there are indeed signs for those who understand." [Surah Aaly Imran, 3:189-90]

Shawana and Sulaiman spent the rest of the afternoon exploring the marketplace, amazed by how numbers played a role in everything. They helped Mustafa weigh spices, calculate prices, and even learned how to use an astrolabe to tell time using the sun and stars!

As the sun began to set, Shawana and Sulaiman knew they had found something special. They shared a passion for knowledge, and their friendship, though new, felt like it could transcend time and place.

THE GOLDEN AGE OF ISLAM

The next few days were a whirlwind of discovery for Shawana and Sulaiman. They explored beyond the bustling marketplace, delving deeper into the world of knowledge that flourished during the Golden Age of Islam.

One morning, Mustafa took them to a magnificent building with towering arches and beautiful mosaics.

"This is the House of Wisdom," he explained. "Scholars from all over the world come here to study and share their knowledge."

At the entrance, a verse from the Quran was inscribed in elegant calligraphy:

"'This is' a blessed Book which We have revealed to you 'O Prophet' so that they may ponder over its verses, and that those endowed with intellects would remind themselves."

[Surah Sad, 38:29]

Inside, Shawana and Sulaiman found themselves in rooms overflowing with books, scrolls, and maps. Scholars huddled in groups, deep in discussion about philosophy, astronomy, medicine, and mathematics. The air buzzed with intellectual energy, and the thirst for knowledge was almost tangible.

They met Al-Khwarizmi, a renowned scholar known as the "father of algebra." He showed them how numbers could be used to solve problems and unlock the secrets of the universe. Shawana was amazed to see how his work formed the basis of the math she was learning back in her own time!

Next, they encountered Ibn Sina, a famous physician and philosopher. He explained how the human body worked, why hygiene and healthy living were so important, and how medicine could be used to ease suffering. Shawana was fascinated by his holistic approach, which considered not just the physical body but also the mind and spirit.

As they explored the House of Wisdom and other centers of learning, Shawana and Sulaiman saw firsthand the incredible contributions Muslim scholars had made to many fields of knowledge. They learned about advancements in astronomy, with intricate instruments like astrolabes used to study the stars and planets. They discovered innovations in engineering, with magnificent mosques and palaces showcasing architectural marvels. They even explored the world of geography, with maps charting faraway lands and trade routes.

Throughout their journey, Shawana and Sulaiman shared their own knowledge and perspectives. Shawana, with her modern scientific background, helped Sulaiman understand complex concepts like gravity, the solar system, and how blood circulates through the human body. Sulaiman, in turn, shared his understanding of Islamic history, the Quran's emphasis on seeking knowledge, and how faith and reason were intertwined during the Golden Age.

Their day was filled with new discoveries and insightful reflections. Shawana's perspective on the world shifted dramatically. She'd always thought of science as a product of the Western world, but now she knew that many nations had contributed to scientific progress over the centuries. She felt a sense of pride knowing that Muslim scholars had played such a vital role.

WHEN FAITH & SCIENCE MEET

One sunny afternoon, as Shawana and Sulaiman were engrossed in a lively discussion about the planets, they overheard a group of men talking nearby. The men's voices were hushed, their faces etched with disapproval.

"Look at those children," one muttered, pointing toward Shawana and Sulaiman. "Wasting their time with worldly knowledge instead of focusing on prayer. It's a shame."

"Indeed," another man chimed in. "They should be memorizing the Quran and learning about the Prophet's life, not fiddling with stars and numbers."

Shawana's heart sank. Their words echoed the doubts she had struggled with back in her own time. The guilt and confusion she thought she had overcome came rushing back.

Sulaiman noticed her change in mood. "Don't listen to them, Shawana," he whispered. "We know that all knowledge is important."

But Shawana couldn't shake off the feeling of unease. She remembered her aunt's words, and the pressure she felt to prioritize religious studies above all else.

"But what if they're right, Sulaiman?" she asked, her voice trembling slightly. "What if learning about science *does* distract us from our faith?"

Sulaiman, though feeling a little unsure himself, put on a brave face. "We need to find answers, Shawana," he said. "Let's ask someone who can help us."

He remembered a wise old scholar they had met at the House of Wisdom, a man known for his vast knowledge of Islam.

Shawana agreed, and together they hurried off to find the scholar. They found him in the courtyard of the mosque, surrounded by students of all ages, eagerly listening to his every word.

Sulaiman approached the scholar respectfully and explained their dilemma. The scholar listened patiently, his kind eyes full of understanding.

"My dear children," he began in a gentle voice, "seeking knowledge is not something to be feared. In fact, it is a duty for every Muslim, as emphasized in the Quran and the teachings of our beloved Prophet Muhammad, peace be upon him."

He recited a verse from the Quran:

"<u>Read</u>! In the Name of your Lord Who has created (all that exists). He has created man from a clot. <u>Read</u>! And your Lord is the Most Generous, Who has taught (the writing) by the pen. He has taught humanity what they knew not."
[Surah Al-'Alaq, 96:1-5]

"This verse," the scholar explained, "was the first revelation received by Prophet Muhammad (P.B.U.H). It emphasizes the importance of reading, learning, and seeking knowledge."

He continued, "The Prophet (P.B.U.H) himself encouraged his followers to seek knowledge, even if they had to travel far and wide to find it."

The Messenger of Allah (P.B.U.H) said:

"Seeking knowledge is a duty upon every Muslim."
[Sunan Ibn Majah, 224]

The scholar shared stories about how the early Muslims valued knowledge and sought it out from different cultures and civilizations. He spoke of great Muslim scholars like Al-Razi, who made important discoveries in medicine, and Ibn Khaldun, who revolutionized the study of history and sociology.

"These scholars, and many others like them, didn't see any conflict between their faith and their pursuit of knowledge," the scholar explained. "They understood that all knowledge ultimately comes from Allah, and that studying His creation is a way to appreciate His wisdom and power."

He looked at Shawana and Sulaiman with a warm smile. "My dear children," he said, "don't let anyone discourage you from seeking knowledge, whether it's about the stars in the sky, the plants on the earth, or the words of the Quran. As long as you use your knowledge for good, to help others and make the world a better place, you are fulfilling your duty as Muslims and walking on the path of righteousness."

Shawana and Sulaiman felt an immense sense of relief upon hearing the scholar's wise words. Their doubts vanished, replaced by a renewed belief that their love of learning was not only compatible with their faith, but an important part of it.

Later that evening, as they sat under a star-filled sky, Sulaiman turned to Shawana and asked, "Do you still feel conflicted about loving both science and Islam?"

Shawana thought for a moment, gazing up at the twinkling stars. "Not anymore," she finally replied. "Seeing how the scholars here embraced all kinds of knowledge as a way to understand Allah's creation has shown me that they don't have to be separate. They actually work together, like two sides of the same coin."

Sulaiman nodded. "Just like Uncle Mustafa said, all knowledge is a gift from Allah (S.W.T)," he said. "And using that knowledge to help others, solve problems, and make the world a better place is a way of worshipping Him."

Shawana smiled, feeling a sense of peace and clarity she had never felt before. Her journey to the Golden Age had done more than just open her eyes to the amazing history of Islamic scholarship; it had helped her resolve the conflict in her own heart.

She realized that her passion for science wasn't separate from her faith; it was a way to connect more deeply with the wonders of Allah's creation. She could use her knowledge to make a positive difference in the world, just like the scholars of the Golden Age had done centuries before.

A FUTURE FILLED WITH STARS

As the days passed, Shawana felt a growing sadness. She loved her time in the Golden Age, exploring and learning alongside Sulaiman. But she knew it was almost time to go home.

One evening, she told Sulaiman how she was feeling. "I miss my family," she confessed. "And I know it's time for me to return."

Sulaiman understood. He would miss their adventures and their exciting discussions, but he knew that Shawana belonged in her own time.

They walked back to the old marketplace, where their journey had begun. Shawana held the astrolabe tightly. Its familiar weight felt comforting now, a reminder of her incredible adventure. As she touched its intricate surface, the world around her began to blur.

Suddenly, she was back in the dusty antique shop, the sounds and smells of the modern marketplace slowly coming back into focus. Her father was standing beside her, his face etched with worry.

"Shawana, where did you go?" he exclaimed, pulling her into a relieved hug. "You just disappeared!"

Shawana looked around, her heart overflowing with emotion. The shop seemed smaller now, less magical than she remembered. But she also saw it in a new light, appreciating the history and stories hidden within each object.

"I had the most amazing adventure, Baba," she said, her voice full of excitement. "I traveled back in time to the Golden Age of Islam, and I learned so much!"

Shawana couldn't wait to tell her family all about her adventure! She described Sulaiman, the kind merchant Mustafa, the incredible House of Wisdom, and the brilliant scholars she had met. She told them about the bustling marketplace, the thirst for knowledge, and how beautifully faith and reason were intertwined during the Golden Age.

Her family listened, their eyes wide with wonder. Even Shawana's aunt, who had cautioned her about focusing too much on science, looked at her with newfound respect.

"Shawana," she said, "your journey sounds incredible! I never realized how much Muslims contributed to science and other fields throughout history. It makes me so proud of our heritage."

Shawana's experience sparked a wave of curiosity and inspiration within her family and community. People started to rediscover the rich history of Islamic scholarship and the importance of seeking knowledge in all its forms. The artificial wall between faith and reason that Shawana had once felt so strongly began to crumble.

Back at school, Shawana pursued her scientific studies with even more passion and confidence. She no longer felt conflicted or guilty. Instead, she saw her love for science as a way to connect with Allah's creation, just like the scholars of the Golden Age. She excelled in her classes, participated in science fairs, and loved sharing her knowledge with others.

Shawana never forgot her journey back in time or the lessons she had learned. She continued to explore the world with an open mind and a curious heart, always seeking new knowledge and using it to make the world a better place.

Years later, Shawana became a famous scientist, making groundbreaking discoveries that helped improve people's lives. But she never forgot the importance of her faith and the values she had learned on her journey to the Golden Age. She remained grounded in her Islamic beliefs, using her knowledge and success to serve humanity and inspire other young Muslims to embrace all forms of knowledge as a way to fulfill their potential and create a brighter future for everyone.

Enter a world where faith meets imagination in this wonderful collection of five Islamic stories. Each tale weaves together **adventure**, **wisdom**, and important **Islamic teachings** to help young Muslims navigate their journey of faith with confidence and joy.

What's Inside This Collection:

"Rashid and the Tapestry of Wonders" - Step through a wonderful tapestry with Rashid as he discovers the beautiful names of Allah through captivating stories that bring Islamic concepts to life.

"Aleena Tames Her Anger Monster" - Join Aleena as she learns to manage her emotions with Islamic teachings, practical techniques, and the loving guidance of her family and community.

"Safiya's Big Change" - Follow a thoughtful caterpillar's transformation as she learns about Paradise and the importance of preparing for the Hereafter through good deeds.

"Friends Fighting Shaytaan's Whispers!" - Meet Omar and his friends in The Conscience Club as they work together to make good choices and resist temptation through friendship and faith.

"Ibrahim Learns the Power of Dua" - Experience the transformative power of prayer with Ibrahim as he discovers that Allah always listens to our sincere supplications, even when answers come in unexpected ways.

This Collection Will Help Children:
- Develop a stronger connection with Allah through understanding His beautiful names
- Learn practical Islamic solutions for everyday challenges
- Understand core Islamic concepts like dua, the Hereafter, and resisting temptation
- Build character through stories about patience, perseverance, and making good choices
- Find comfort in Allah's presence during times of difficulty

Perfect For:
- Muslim children ages 5-11
- Islamic schools and weekend madrasas
- Family reading time and bedtime stories
- Building a foundation of Islamic knowledge through engaging storytelling